An Energy Drink For The Soul

"The 1st Sip"

By

Jennifer L. Dean

ISBN: 1-4140-2304-9 (e-book)
ISBN: 1-4140-2303-0 (Paperback)

This book is printed on acid-free paper.

1stBooks – rev. 11/21/03

Dedication

My book is only dedicated to God with whom all things are possible.

Thanks

I must thank my husband, Mike, and my daughter, Tiffany, for their excellent writing skills. I would also like to thank my parents, my son Aundre, my other daughter Shannon and my family and friends for their love, support, and inspiration. A special thanks to all who attended my seminars and workshops, because each person left a special part of themselves with me. Additionally, a special thanks to my editor Ms. Sammie Justesen for all of her help in making my dream a reality.

Table of Contents

Dedication..iii

Introduction..vii

Why So Much Drama?...1

How You See Life is How Life Sees You 13

Life 101: The Basics 21

Roller Coaster or Merry-Go-Round?......................27

Don't Beat a Dead Horse...35

Dreams 45

Let's Get Back to Basics...51

Restricted for reader under 18................................59

The Quicksand of Life..67

Conclusion..71

About the Author...73

Introduction

I've long awaited the time when I could put some of my thoughts in writing. Finally, that time has come. This book contains short essays about life and ways we can get through it, knowing "this to shall pass." I'm excited about sharing my philosophy of life with you.

I see life as something you make for yourself, never blaming others or making excuses for why you are where you are. **Life is neither fair nor unfair – it's exactly what you make it**. What you get out of life will be equal to what you put into it. If you can learn to put joy into your life, then you can stay connected to that joy every moment of the day.

Life is short. Some of us get to live a long time, while others leave early, but many people never really appreciate the time we have. Remember, each day might be your last. What would you like to say and do on your last day? Have you lived your life to the fullest?

God gives each of us special talents and a special purpose in life. Let go of the hurts, anger, and traumas that keep you from doing your best and living up to your full potential. Go after life, live with passion, get in touch with your creativity, and find out why you're here!

May God bless each of you as you embrace life.

Why So Much Drama?

If you find yourself constantly bouncing from one dramatic situation to another, it might be time to evaluate your life. Have you ever thought about why we have so much drama in our lives? I know people who seem to have a dark cloud following them everywhere they go. They're so wrapped up in the tornadoes of their own lives that they have little time for anyone else. And they love to drag other people into the storm. A tornado picks up everything and everyone in its path and dumps them where it darn well pleases. It isn't much fun to have a life filled with tornadoes.

Webster's Dictionary defines drama as "a state, situation, or series of events involving interesting or intense conflict of forces." J. Dean's dictionary says, "Drama is any excess baggage that causes personal chaos that spills out of control and can ultimately lead to havoc and chaos."

You should be aware of the baggage you're storing, especially if it sometimes develops into major drama that affects not only your life, but also the people around you. Take a few minutes and list 5 areas of your life that are about to spill over into drama:

1.
2.

3.

4.

5.

Everyone has baggage as a part of life, and each of us carries different bags with different weights. Sometimes I think we should put a limit on the bags we can bring on board our lives, as they do when we fly on the airline. Only 2 per passenger and only one carry-on baggage that will fit in the overhead bins. Otherwise things become unbalanced, too much for one person to carry.

Take a good look at the baggage you listed above before we begin the "spring cleaning" process. How many of these issues were caused by impulsive decisions on your part? Are some of them due to lack of planning? Do you have chaotic relationships in your life that you need to rethink?

Is there a dark cloud overhead?

Sometimes fate just seems to throw hurdles at our feet as we try to race through life. Some of us encounter speed bumps, potholes, and manholes. Other people encounter the Rocky Mountains! Are you one of those folks who has a dark cloud following you through life? And I don't mean ordinary gray clouds, I mean purplish-black clouds that seem to produce a major downpour of emotions.

Many people don't understand that drama is a personal choice and can become a habit. Life changes as much as the weather; it can be beautiful and sunny one moment and rainy the next. By looking at the brighter side of life, you can turn an 80% chance of rain into a 20% chance of sunshine. Don't constantly feed the "**drama monster**." Your goal is to change "mostly cloudy" to "partly cloudy," and then to "not a cloud in the sky." It all depends on how you approach your problems. *And maybe, just maybe, the dark cloud you see overhead is a reflection of the dark clouds inside you.*

Do you have areas of you life where there's too much rain? Rain helps the flowers grow, but it can also wash them away. I've had that feeling many times in my life. I always tell myself, "Just hang on. This storm won't last forever and then the sun will shine again." Only in Biblical times did it rain for 40 days and nights, and then God had a specific purpose in mind.

Impulsive decisions lead to DRAMA

Are you falling into a wormhole and feel as though you're part of "One Life to Live" or "As the World Turns" or maybe "The Young and The Restless?" Do you find yourself facing the same old problems? How would your life change for the better if you didn't have to deal with these situations? Maybe it's time to change your role in life from Drama Queen to Happily Ever After.

Ironically, difficult situations often turn out to be things we've invited into our lives. Many people bring drama on themselves, or get swept into other people's dramas without considering the consequences.

In the heat of conflict we humans tend to make impulsive decisions we later regret. What about buying an expensive car when you know you'll have trouble making the monthly payments? What about the impulsive decision to call in sick for work just because you don't want to go in? How about the bad decision to drive home after you've had too much to drink? Decisions like these can have far-reaching consequences that sometimes take a lifetime to repair. Sometimes we lose things that are irreplaceable. What are three biggest decisions you've made the last 10 years?

1.

2.

3.

- Do you feel you made the best possible choices?
- Were any of these decisions impulsive? How did they turn out?
- Would you make different choices, given the 20/20 vision of hindsight?

The next time you're faced with an important decision, take time to weigh the options and consider how different choices might influence your future. List the pros and cons on two sides of a sheet of paper. This is a simple, but effective way to reduce drama in your life.

Anxiety leads to DRAMA

Anxiety is a product of excessive worrying which can cause drama. If you've ever had an anxiety attack, you know it's an overwhelming sense of apprehension and fear, often accompanied by sweating, nausea, a racing pulse, and cold, clammy hands. Some people go through life in a constant state of anxiety that blossoms into a full fledged anxiety attack when problems arise. Generalized anxiety disorder (GAD) affects over 19 million Americans. From 55 to 66 percent of people with this disorder are female.

The focus of generalized anxiety often shifts, usually focusing on things like finances, health, your job, and family. But the intensity of the worry is always out of proportion to the actual problems at hand. A small amount of anxiety is good, it keeps you on your toes. But too much anxiety is bad for your health and leads to excess drama in your life.

Take a few minutes to list things that bring you anxiety:

1.

2.

3.

4.

5.

Are your worries reasonable or exaggerated? Do they affect other aspects of your life and keep you awake at night?

Chaotic relationships lead to DRAMA

Unlike anxiety, chaotic relationships are never beneficial. They always lead to drama, and many people find themselves living in the eye of the storm, unsure how to get out. In addition to causing drama, chaotic relationships are detrimental to your mental and physical health. They often lead to illness, depression, and anxiety attacks. They cause your life to become an emotional mess, taking away from your priorities. Soon your life starts to resemble the bedroom of a teenage boy who's retaliating against his parents. Take a few minutes and list the relationships that bring chaos into your life. Be honest with yourself and take a close look at these bags you carry with you:

1.

2.

3.

4.

5.

It isn't easy getting out of a chaotic relationship, especially if the relationship involves physical and/or mental abuse. Don't expect your friends, coworkers, or family to come to the rescue. Instead, seek professional help.

Have you become part of someone else's life drama? For example, some people continuously let relatives, coworkers, or friends take advantage of them. If you're always loaning people money and bailing them out of trouble, it might be time to make a clean sweep and get these unhealthy relationships out of your life.

Excess baggage

Have you ever rushed to catch a plane with a heavy suitcase in one hand, a garment bag draped over your shoulder, and a carry-on bag in your other hand? Some of us go through life the same way, encumbered by baggage that keeps us from living up to our full potential. We can barely make it over the bumps and potholes of life, much less climb mountains.

But we CAN learn to pack more efficiently. We have to start by reducing the size of the bag and the amount of baggage, then prioritize what we're willing to carry.

Baggage types

- Some of us have bags we've been lugging around most of our lives. Remember those small brown paper sacks we used as children to carry lunch? Sometimes those sacks still seem to linger from our past.

7

- Some of us have invested in the very expensive luggage: Coach Luggage to hold our baggage. People who fall into this category like to dress their problems up and flaunt them as assets. Not wanting to let go of the baggage, they choose to carry it in style.

- The worst type of baggage has to be the extra-large Hefty garbage bags filled with litter and waste. These bags emit terrible odors and are the heaviest to drag along. They're filled with situations that turned ugly, an ugly mix of anxiety, impulsive decisions, and chaotic relationships all thrown in together.

Reclaiming your baggage

One thing you must remember is that life continually changes and shifts. When removing baggage from the overhead bin in an airplane the stewardess always reminds us to be extra careful, because cargo tends to shift during the flight. And so it is with life. If you aren't careful, your baggage (or someone else's) can end up hitting you on the head as you try to remove it.

At the baggage claim area in the airport you'll see people and bags of many different colors, shapes, and sizes. Your bags contain your personal life. Don't make the mistake of picking up someone else's baggage, and don't offer yours to them.

Let's gather up the trash!

Picture yourself getting ready to set your trash out for the garbage man. You only have one day a week that's designated as trash day, so it's important to have everything ready. It's time to release and let go!

It's time to unpack those closet skeletons. I mean the things you've classified Top Secret, never shared with anyone. These are secrets you've kept all your life, never telling anyone about them. This closet is sealed like the tombs of the Egyptian pharaohs, never to be opened. Everyone, no matter their race, gender, or position in life, has skeletons in the closet. These secrets can be the heaviest baggage of all, weighing us down like chains around our ankles as we go through life.

No matter how small the bones, those skeletons can eventually fill a dreaded Hefty bag. When the bag becomes too heavy and begins to rip, bones fall out and the drama begins. It's time to take a close look at our baggage.

It's also time to unpack the hurts and resentments you've carried around for years. People you haven't forgiven. Anger you've stored away. Frustration and jealousy you can't let go of. Use a shovel if you must, but drag these bags from your closet and expose them to the light. Cultivate forgiveness.

If you can't forgive, at least learn to let go of the baggage so you can move on with your life.

When to unpack the bags

Yes, you may need to unpack some of your bags and examine the contents before you throw them out with the trash. But we have to choose when and where to unpack.

At work? Absolutely not! Despite the gossip that floats around almost every workplace in America, this isn't the place to unpack your bags. I know the urge is there, because your extra-friendly coworkers may seem interested and helpful. They act sympathetic and are always there for you when you come in acting emotionally drained. In truth, what they're looking for is new gossip. Becoming a hot topic for office gossip is the quickest way to bring new drama into your life.

Don't even take your bags inside the workplace. Leave them at the door when you enter. That means don't come to work looking emotionally drained, no matter how bad you feel. Put a smile on your face and a positive attitude in your pocket as you walk through the door. And when it's time to leave, I promise, those bags will be waiting for you at the door.

You also don't want to become a burden or an object of pity to your family, friends, and coworkers. These people will show their support, but too much negativity will eventually lead those same people to avoid you because you bring them down.

Setting out the trash

Now that you've privately unpacked your baggage, cleaned the closets, and brushed away the cobwebs, it's time to set out the trash. You may have *real* items to throw away, such as photos, letters, and other stuff you've been hanging onto. You'll also have piles of baggage and clutter from your mind. Visualize dumping all these items into a black plastic garbage bag, made extra tough to hold everything.

This isn't easy. It may take awhile to get rid of everything, and you may choose to do it a little at a time. But when you're ready, seal that Hefty bag, drag it to the curb, and then watch the garbage truck haul it away.

How You See Life is How Life Sees You

Looking in the mirror, you see a reflection of yourself, and this mirror image is your life looking back at you. You may not always like what you see in the mirror, but if you want to improve your life it's a good place to start.

Recently I looked in the mirror and noticed a few signs of aging. I have graying hair, wrinkles, and crow's feet around my eyes. Instead of letting the aging process depress me, I choose to make the best of it. After all, I'm not getting older, I'm getting better!

Age is only a Number

We have all met 16 year olds who act as though they're 30, and 30 year old people who act 16. I believe age is relative to your attitude and the experiences you've chosen as you move through life. At the age of 40, I've already lived through half the average life span for a human being. I can't change anything that happened in the past, but I can take my experiences and build on them.

It has been projected that by 2006, 1 in 3 North Americans will be over the age of 50. As the huge baby boom generation moves up the age ladder, the youth culture ideals of the 1960's are shifting to concerns of a more mature nature, such as planning for the future. I plan on living at least another 40 years, so I have to prepare and get ready for those years by looking to the future and considering my next move.

As we get older, most of us are forced to admit we haven't reached the lofty goals we set for ourselves. But that doesn't matter. Somehow along the way we've learned the things we need to know. Many people go into panic mode at a certain age when they have to give up their dreams. This can bring on a major depression if you begin to doubt your self-worth, so it's important to remember that each stage of life brings its own rewards. You may not have the energy or stamina of a 20 year old, but you've gained wisdom and experience. Many people have started second careers and achieved their full potential after the age of 50.

Accept the fact that everyone ages, but growing older doesn't mean you have to sit in a rocking chair for the next 50 years. If you don't feel your age, there's no rule saying you have to act it, regardless of what other people think. Be yourself! One of the best things about getting older is the realization that what other people think doesn't matter as much as you thought when you were younger. As a strong, independent adult you can now set your own course in life.

If you tend to focus on things you haven't done in life, this is a good time to celebrate the things you <u>have</u> accomplished. Make a list of your achievements, and don't forget to include such things as raising children, taking care of your family, and acquiring good friends:

1.

2.

3.

4.

5.

Consider these verses from Jenny's Joseph's well know poem, "When I Am An Old Woman I Shall Wear Purple:"

When I am an old woman I shall wear purple
With a red hat which doesn't go, and doesn't suit me.
    And I shall spend my pension on brandy and summer gloves
And satin sandals, and say we've no money for butter.

I shall sit down on the pavement when I'm tired
And gobble up samples in shops and press alarm bells
    And run my stick along the public railings
And make up for the sobriety of my youth.

Each of us has a "magic age" and we suffer pangs of regret when this year passes and we haven't achieved everything we set out to do. But remember, age is only a number!

Life Is What You Make It

Many times I've asked myself why I was chosen to own a company God so graciously blessed me with. He placed it in my hands 12 years ago, but He expected me to put something into it also: Hard work! When all is said and done, the results I achieve with my company are not due to good luck or bad luck, they're based on how hard I'm willing to work.

Life is exactly what you make it. If you put forth 150% effort, you'll get back exactly what you put in. This holds true for jobs, relationships, parenting, school, and every other aspect of our lives. If you wait until the last minute to do everything, you get last minute results.

I often ask people in my seminars: "If you worked on a straight commission with no salary, would you be more motivated than you are now?" Most people complain about working too hard and not receiving enough compensation for the hours they put in. But if the tables were turned and your earnings were based exactly on how much work you accomplished, how would your work habits change? Most people say they'd prefer to keep getting a regular paycheck based on a rate they've agreed on with their employer.

However, I remind people that they actually are working on a form of commission, because once their sick days and vacation time are used up, the company will start deducting missed time from their checks. And eventually there will be no check.

Attitude

I recently visited a friend who was diagnosed with cancer, expecting him to be sad and depressed about the illness. To my surprise, he was upbeat and told me, "This is something I have to live with. It may not be what kills me, but my life isn't over yet and I'm going to live every day of it."

My friend knows every day is an opportunity. He could have said, "Life isn't fair." He could've asked, "Why me?" But he believes everything happens for a reason and the cancer will make him stronger, and a better person because of his trials. This man is one of my heroes, because he believes he can over come this and anything else that comes his way in life. He knows God has a reason for everything that happens, and He can do anything but fail. When you have this mighty army fighting your battles, there's no way to lose. When you come through it you will be a better, stronger person.

How Does Life See You?

> Fires can't be made with dead embers, nor can enthusiasm be stirred by spiritless men. Enthusiasm in our daily work lightens effort and turns even labor into pleasant tasks. — James Baldwin

Do you have a "boring" job? Do you drag through each day, complaining about how life treats you? Did you ever stop to think that how you see life is how life sees you? As you gaze into the mirror, perhaps that mirror looks back. List five ways you see your life right now:

1.

2.

3.

4.

5.

If you find yourself trapped by circumstances and "bad luck," consider how you can assume more responsibility for your life. Believing someone else is in charge of everything and you have no choice will leave you depressed and bitter about the cards you've been dealt. If something in your life isn't working and you're waiting for someone else to come along and change it, you'd best not hold your breath! Life gives back what you put into it.

List five ways you can change the "man in the mirror:"

1.

2.

3.

4.

5.

We build our lives a day at a time: What kind of building materials do you want to use? Your attitudes and the choices you make today will influence how you live ten years from now. As you consider the changes you'd like to make, set mini-goals for yourself that will lead you toward the ultimate vision. These conscious choices you make along the way will determine your lifetime path. Life is not meant to be a struggle and bring unhappiness. God wants us to be happy, but we must learn to look at the person in the mirror and decide who we want to see and eventually be.

Life is exactly what you make of it, so get out there and stop making excuses. God gave each of us a life. It may not be fair, but it's all we have and it's ours!

Life 101: The Basics

Watch for the Warning Signs

Meteorologists can predict when a tornado may form because they recognize the warning signs and have researched the patterns of tornadoes. Sometimes they announce conditions are favorable for a tornado. When one is actually spotted, the watch becomes a tornado warning.

We need to research the patterns of our lives and become aware when there's a tornado watch or warning. I must say, sometimes I've ignored warning signs. I've seen black clouds forming on the horizon and thought, "we may get some rain," when it turned out to be an F5 tornado. We should try and recognize these warning signs so we can avoid as many of the storms of life as possible.

Do you habitually ignore or deny these signals? What are you pretending not to know? Pick a simple event in your life where something bad happened to you, then go back in time and analyze the situation. Did your own action (or lack of action) have something to do with the end result? Perhaps you ignored certain clues that told you this particular tornado was brewing in your life. Next time, like a good meteorologist, learn to predict the storm and take evasive action before it hits.

Who's in Charge?

Have you ever told yourself you wouldn't do something – like finish that last piece of chocolate cake, and then you end up doing it anyway? Addictions are another example. We may tell ourselves, "This is my last cigarette and then I'm going to quit," but all too often the craving is stronger than our will power.

Perhaps you find yourself making the same mistakes over and over. Making a mistake the first time is understandable, but making it twice is a bad choice. You can learn and grow from mistakes, but repeating them shows you didn't learn anything. Wake up and realize that if you're a repeat offender you've fallen into what I call the habit stage, a black hole, and you have to stop yourself. This isn't an easy process, but it's something you'll have to do in order to move forward.

You may have to choose new friends, stay away from certain family members, and even change jobs. Remember, **who you're around is who you become**. Where you focus is where you go. You must change your focus in life in order to change your path. A new path equals new results.

I waged an internal battle about eating late at night. I had to tell myself, "Now listen, you're not 16 any more, you're 40, and your body doesn't treat food the way it used to. If you eat this now you'll be wearing it tomorrow."

I also have internal battles about other people. I've always been a pleaser, so I've had to train myself to say no and stand up for what's right. I've learned to analyze my motives before I agree to do things.

When you're faced with such decisions, ask yourself, "Who's in charge of this life, me or my habits?"

Parenting: One of the Most Important Jobs on Earth

Our children didn't ask us to bring them into this world, but we made the decision to have them. As they grow, their actions affect their peers, their elders, and us as parents. If children are exposed to wrong decisions and bad examples, it's only natural for them to copy their environment. These children will ultimately take the wrong decisions and bad examples they learned at home out into the world, including school and their workplaces.

We live in a society where citizens, neighbors, and community members must deal with a parent's decision not to parent their children. Teachers aren't placed in the schools to raise our children, their job is to educate. We can't expect the schools to take on a job we've refused to do.

Parenting isn't easy. It's like marriage, a day to day process. We have to pray for guidance, direction, and strength. We can't quit, and we shouldn't take our frustrations out on our children. I realize this is sometimes easier said than done, but it's well worth the effort. No matter what they say, our children

23

need and want discipline in their lives. It's an individual choice how you discipline your children, but without it your kids will be raising themselves and making decisions they aren't equipped to handle.

And yes, this does affect all of us!

Give Yourself a Tune Up

Every once in awhile I realize that, like a car, I've gone over my mileage and my maintenance light is on. I recently told my daughter she had too many miles on her car since the last oil change. She protested at first, but eventually took the car in for servicing. The mechanic told her if she'd waited another day or two she would've burned out the engine.

If we don't occasionally get our minds and bodies tuned up, we may burn out just like the engine in that car. Can you list five things you've done for yourself over the past few months?

1.
2.
3.
4.
5.

If you're so busy taking care of your job and other people that you haven't been caring for yourself, then it's definitely time for a tune up. Here are some suggestions to simplify your life:

- Take a class in something you enjoy

- Develop a new hobby or interest
- Treat yourself to a nice meal and an evening out.
- Have a weekend retreat at home
- Pamper yourself at a spa
- Get a massage and a new hairstyle
- Do something different, something you use to love to do but stopped

Viewing your mind, body, and spirit as a fine automobile that requires periodic maintenance can help reduce the guilt you feel about spending time and money on yourself. Your engine will purr if you give it a tune up!

Roller Coaster or Merry-Go-Round?

During the past year I've gone through so many learning experiences that my life often felt like a roller coaster. Sometimes it's rough handling all the loops, corkscrews, and acceleration of the world's biggest and scariest roller coaster, life. Even though everyone is safely buckled in, you're stomach churns with excitement and fear as the ride begins. The cars move slowly at first, traveling upward on a steep grade with only the sky visible ahead. With each click of the wheels you know the drop is coming. The thrill is beyond words as you peer over the side and see your friends waving from below. Finally, after what seems like eternity, the roller coaster reaches the top. Although you still can't see the drop, you know it's just ahead. The cars pause for a few seconds, balance precariously, and then plunge downward like a tidal wave in the ocean.

The first wave of the roller coaster is over, but your ride has just begun. Before you recover from the initial scare you're zooming over the track at top speed, thrust up and down, and twisted from side to side. When the cars are hanging upside down you wonder why you ever bought a ticket in the first place.

That's how I felt the year my husband bought me Taekwondo lessons as a Christmas present. I was elated, this was something I'd always wanted to try and I'd never done anything like it. At the age of 36, my mind was ready for a new challenge. It didn't occur to me that my 36 year old body might have other ideas.

From the first lesson on, I had to get used to the idea of being taught by and saying "Yes sir!" to someone half my age. I realized early on that I was going to have to bend, twist, and mold myself into shape. At my age everything on my body told me to quit, from my feet to my fingers. My body screamed for relief for almost 2 weeks, but I wouldn't give up. I knew it was a case of mind over matter, and I had to convince my mind to motivate my body.

It was like being on the rollercoaster that started out nice and slow, but as the class started to pick up speed, things got harder. I felt totally uncoordinated, and we only had six weeks to prepare for the first belt test. During the test, each student has three chances to get it right. I thought my first two tries were okay, but I messed up the third one. I cried all the way home, because I was sure I hadn't passed. I was disappointed in myself and really embarrassed to go inside, so I sat in the car awhile, talking to myself. Boy, what a rollercoaster ride that day was! Finally I had to end my pity party and tell myself, "Suck it up and get over it." I received my next belt the following week. Sometimes we allow our emotions to drive our thoughts and our actions.

In spite of everything, I refused to give up. I had to retrain my body to practice, so I started working out with my kids, my husband, my employees, and everyone else I met. My instructor said to practice in the car and on my way to work. I followed his advice because I wanted to be the best, even at 36 years old.

Before I passed my first belt test I was diagnosed with osteoporosis, meaning my bones were extremely porous and subject to fractures. Not only would my bones break easily, but they were slow to heal and I was at risk for curvature of the spine as the vertebrae in my back collapsed. At the age of 36, I had the bones of a 70 year old woman. I felt as though the roller coaster of life had passed right over me! I felt like giving up and sitting on the sidelines, but instead I got back on the ride.

Every time I walked through the door people in class would stare at me as if to say, "Is she back again?" My instructor said, "You just don't give up, do you?"

He was right. After two knee surgeries and two broken bones in my foot, I finally passed the test for my first degree black belt.

Have there been challenges in your life that felt like roller coasters? List five twists, turns, and bends you've taken that helped mold you into the enthusiastic, energy-driven person you want to be:

1.

2.

3.

4.

5.

At the age of 40, I recently started working out. I joined a local gym and went to Jenny Craig to get the proper food until I could learn about how and what to eat. Now I truly respect anyone who's lost weight by following a life-changing plan. The difficulty of this took me completely by surprise. I've had to keep myself in check and look deep inside to find the self-discipline I needed. I also learned I should've started this better eating/exercise thing earlier in life. However, **anyone can be a shoulda, woulda, coulda**. I should have, I would have, but only talking and never doing. Don't consistently talk about something you will do, it won't happen. Just get off you butt and do it! Make up your mind, look deep inside, gather all the determination in there, and go for it!

Making myself learn new eating habits and exercising is a challenge. I sometimes feel like staying where I am would be easier for me, and for the people around me. But something inside says, "Girl, get out there and move! Go for it!"

Now I'm finally on the road to a healthier, more productive life. As my grandmother said, "Everything that comes easy ain't always good for you."

I often tell people that **habits are easy to start and very hard to break.** Sometimes I feel as though I have two minds. One says, "Stay put and you'll be just fine." The other urges me to move on, face new challenges, and keep pushing forward.

The question: would you rather ride the roller coaster with all its ups and downs or stay on the merry go round where nothing changes? Change is good for the soul.

Like many business owners in this country, after the events of 9-11 I had to look at making changes personally and professionally. The Houston market had just suffered a disastrous tropical storm and we lost one of our offices in the flood. Then the tragedy of 9-11 struck, making things even worse. I had to look at my position in life and in the company and ask God for direction. The pressure of the economy really hit our company hard; as I am sure it did many others. I had to bend, twist, and drag myself to accept the situation, and then be willing to adapt. Slowly, I learned to bend and mold myself into a better person, and through all the stress and anxiety I learned many valuable lessons about myself and business. God took me back to basics and forced me to start from the beginning. He placed many talented business professionals in my path that had faith in what we had done for the past 10 years. They gave us advice, direction, and were there with us when the battles were raging.

By definition, growth requires change. Sometimes God prunes our lives the way we'd prune an unruly plant in the garden, cutting away nonproductive limbs so new and vital growth can appear. If you've spent years on a merry-go-round, making changes in your life can be like stepping onto a roller coaster. You may need to give up certain habits, beliefs, and ways of doing things.

If you find yourself stuck in a rut with outdated habits that no longer fit, spend some time thinking about ways you can do things differently. Open your life to the possibility of change. Welcome new thoughts, feelings, sensations, and friendships. Learn to let go and let God mold you and make you.

What circumstances or events in your life have you learned the most from?

1.

2.

3.

4.

5.

Of these five events, which did you consider negative at the time? How many of them involved drastic changes in your life? Isn't your life better because of what you learned?

As you go through the ups and downs on the roller coaster of life, try seeing God's hand behind the problems you face. Re-think circumstances you've regarded as negative and see how you can use each one as a step to inner growth. Try meeting life as though there are no problems. There are only opportunities for growth and leaning. If you focus on the problem you can't find the solution. Bring solutions along when you think through a problem and focus on what you can do to make things better. Try to control your thoughts. Say aloud, "I am in control of my mind."

I know there was a reason for me to start the Taekwondo program, difficult as it was. If I hadn't begun exercising I might not have discovered my osteoporosis and I shutter to think where I could be now.

Don't ever give up, even when life feels like a roller coaster ride. Just fasten your seatbelt, hold on tight, scream when you need to, and you'll eventually come to the end of the ride.

Don't Beat a Dead Horse

I don't know how many people I've met who harbor ill feelings about someone from the past. Something happened 15 years ago, and we still hate that person. I can truly say I now live a fuller life because I've learned to get off that horse. If the horse is dead, just get off it.

I've encountered many cruel, sloppy, advantageous and criminal people who have taken advantage of me or my company in the past. I am sure I will encounter some of the same type of characters in the future. I remember being young and getting beat up by bullies at school. I won't tell you that doesn't still affect me, but I'm not holding onto it. I don't hold ill feelings toward these people. There have been many times where I have been, talked about, cheated on, misused, abused, and simply treated like I wasn't human. Fortunately, I held on to these problems only for a few minutes, and then I moved on. You should examine the warning signs and remember the patterns. I realize that **holding on to these things will hold me back.** If I don't let go, I can't move forward. I could get stuck with the people who've done me wrong, and then I'd be no better than they are. No one should want that! It's almost like drinking poison yourself and then expecting the other person to die.

Jennifer L. Dean

Anger and Pain

Let me be the first to tell you: holding on to anger and pain inside **only** hurts **YOU**. Anger is a natural human emotion, nature's way of empowering us to ward off an attack or threat to our well being. The problem isn't anger itself; the problem is our mismanagement of anger. Mismanaged anger and rage is a major cause of conflict in our personal and professional relationships. Sometimes we carry anger around for years until it becomes a smoldering fire that flares up over insignificant things. We take it out on people around us; not realizing hidden anger from the past is spilling over and damaging relationships in the present. Holding this anger inside uses precious energy that could be used for other things.

Stop right now and make a list of any people you're harboring anger and resentment against or anything else:

1.
2.
3.
4.
5.

These are the people you need to forgive. It may not happen overnight and you may not be able to do it alone. Many books, tapes, and seminars are available to help, and in some cases you may need the insight of a professional counselor.

36

For serious things, such as physical and emotional abuse, forgiveness can take years to accomplish. Don't rush the process, but never give up. Extinguish those fires! You can do it!

Hidden Anger Leads to Depression

Unexpressed anger can lead to feelings of sadness and depression that can take control of your mind and body. I experienced this and had to make up my mind to either **depress or express**. There was no in-between. Learning to communicate my feelings was a difficult process for me. Don't get me wrong – I could always talk – but I never really said the things I needed to say. I wasn't good at expressing what was on the inside. I was **depressing**, not **expressing**.

I had to learn the hard way to **communicate effectively** with the people who most needed to hear what I had to say. We often tell others how we feel, but find it difficult to share our feelings with the person who really needs to hear them. Complaining about people behind their backs doesn't remove our feelings. In fact, it makes us harbor even more sadness and anger as we dwell on these negative feelings without ever getting rid of them. In my case, sadness led to physical problems, including headaches, chest pains, and ulcers.

Most of the depression starts on the inside where you can't see it developing, and then over the years it works its way to the surface by way of physical problems. I realize dealing with stressful situations is sometimes very difficult and depressing, but it's the only way we move our problems out of the way. You can depress things on a temporary bases, but remember – when you press something down it will eventually erupt, sometimes packing a powerful punch. List three things you should express and not depress:

1.
2.
3.

Remember, the rule is to channel this energy into something that's more beneficial to you. Write a sentence describing how you can release and let go of your sadness and anger:

_____

_____

_____

Letting Go of the Past

It won't be possible for you to have healthy new relationships until you've healed and let go of the hurts from your past. Both your mind and your body will be healthier if you stop harboring negative feelings. Research has shown that people can heal both emotionally *and* physically by forgiving those who've harmed them. According to Samuel D. Standard, a research fellow at Stanford University:

When we are particularly angry about an event over a long period of time, there is often a psychological cost in terms of stress, hostility, strained relationships and so forth. But there is a physical cost as well. When we're especially agitated we produce cortisol, a body chemical, which can help us rally and gain brief strength over a threat. However, an elevated level of cortisol for a prolonged period is implicated in several serious diseases, including diabetes, hypertension, and cancer.

Harboring anger produces a constant flood of stress chemicals that can harm many different parts of the body and lead to things such as headaches, depression, digestion problems, anxiety, heart attacks, and strokes. Is this what you want for yourself?

Think of forgiveness as a **gift to yourself**. You aren't doing it for the other person; you're doing it to free yourself from a heavy burden. Ask yourself, "Am I willing to endanger my health and waste any more energy on this matter?" If the answer is "no," then you're on the path to forgiveness. You can start slowly unwrapping your gift.

Forgiveness Isn't Forgetting

You've probably heard the phrase "forgive and forget," but that isn't really what forgiveness is about. You can't forget the past, nor should you even try, because that would mean giving up the valuable lessons you learned. The real trick is to let go of the past while keeping your eye on the future.

Forgiving someone doesn't mean we condone what they have done to us. We don't have to embrace the deed or make excuses for the person who caused hurt; we just forgive them and move on with our lives. You don't even have to let the person who hurt you off the hook. If he or she committed a criminal act, they should still be punished according to the law. But it isn't your responsibility to grant absolution. That power belongs only to God. The person who hurt you must make his or her own restitution and seek forgiveness from a higher power. If you can forgive and let go, you're taking yourself out of the loop.

Some people say forgiveness is a sign of weakness and that you're inviting people to walk all over you. Actually, the opposite is true. The ability to forgive is a sign of **inner strength and courage**. We give up the crutch of anger we've hidden behind, or the sword of resentment we used to protect ourselves. We stop beating that dead horse and give it a decent burial. These things are replaced by inner peace and security. I have experienced the peace that passes all understanding. When you think you can't go any further, just take one more step.

Have you ever met a professional victim? Some people go through life clinging to hurts and injuries from childhood, letting past events color their present and the future. They use the past as an excuse to keep from interacting with others. Sometimes people who've been hurt use anger to keep others at a distance. Those who dwell on past injuries are still under the control of the people who hurt them.

If you see yourself as a victim, try saying: "I'm sick of this pain and I want to be healed." It may take time and a lot of hard work, but you can recover.

What Forgiveness Means

Letting go of the past is a big part of forgiveness. You can't (and shouldn't) try to erase what happened to you, but you *can* accept it and move on. Don't let pain from your past dictate how you live today and how you'll face the future. You may have to give up on the idea of punishing the person who did you wrong. Dreaming about making someone suffer for what they did only drags you down with negative thoughts and feelings. Would hurting the other person really make you heal? You might feel better for awhile, but true healing comes from within, not from outside events. Give up thoughts of vengeance and move on with your life. Hanging onto the past is like carrying around one of those big Hefty garbage bags we talked about in Chapter 1, toss this bag into the trash along with your other garbage!

Can you run from the past? Not really. You can't run forever, and the past has a way of catching up with us when we least expect it. Forgiveness lets you deal honestly with the past instead of running from it.

When it comes right down to it, each of us has at least one big issue in our lives that we have to deal with. If you placed more than two or three names on the list of people you need to forgive, then forgiveness probably IS a big issue for you. Letting go of this anger will make you a healthier and happier person.

List the first steps you can take to forgive each person on your list.

1.

2.

3.

4.

5.

Where will you begin? It's time to get off your high horse and let go of things that are holding you back. The International Forgiveness Institute (www.forgiveness-institute.org) states that forgiveness is ". . . the foregoing of resentment or revenge when the wrongdoer's actions deserve it and giving the gifts of mercy, generosity and love when the wrongdoer does not deserve them." It's a way of overcoming bad with good. It's a moral response to an immoral act. As we give the gift of forgiveness, we ourselves are healed.

So, if the horse is dead get off of it. **Don't beat a dead horse**. Release and let go of your hurt and anger so you can experience the powerful gifts of life that await you. Learn to communicate effectively by talking to the person who needs to hear what you have to say. When you do this you're no longer trying to put a band-aide on a gushing wound – you're learning to slowly stitch up the wound so you can begin to heal.

Dreams

Dreams are only good when they are chased down and made reality. God doesn't allow us to dream dreams we can't achieve. We just have to move through time and space and we're there. Dream big, because you can do it!

"A dream is a wish your heart makes."

I often think about life, dreaming about what I want to be in 10 years. You know, maybe a surgeon, a lawyer, or owning the best restaurant in Houston. Dreaming is the key to our unconscious mind. It's a tunnel that brings access to see our innermost feelings and needs. Dreams are a reflection of our past and present lives. How we live will show up clearly in our nightmares and our dreams.

When I was younger I wanted to be around people who, in my eyes, were going places and doing things. They gave off an electric energy. But I learned that just because people talk all the time about their dreams doesn't mean they'll make these things happen. Some people are just sleep walking; they don't have the drive or ability to wake up and do something with their dreams.

It's important to choose your friends wisely, because they become part of your dreams. Do your friends support you, offer good advice, and tell you when you've gone off track? When I think about my friends, I think of good things. They're proud of me when I succeed and they encourage me when I fail. At times I've thought, "I don't have the education, the smarts, the finances, or the support to get this done." But my friends said, "You're too close to stop now. Keep trying and you'll succeed!" Identify the people in your life who will help you plant and water your dreams.

1.

2.

3.

Day Dreaming

I actually think day dreams are the best kind of dreams we can have. Right in the middle of the day with everything going on all around us, we just stop and God gives us a dream. Recently I was driving down a beautiful street lined with trees and million dollar houses. I heard God say, "Pick one! Any one you want! If you ask, you can receive it. If you can dream it, it can be a reality."

I do dream big, don't I? I dream of having my own restaurant soon, and I have everything all picked out. I've talked so much about this dream that my kids are starting to make plans for it. I dream big because I *want* big things. And I know there's never a dream God gives me that I can't receive. God will not give me a dream that I can't achieve; I've learned this over and over again. Getting there can be tough, but the end result is the best feeling in the world.

If you have a dream, let it be a big one. Day dreams are important because they put us in touch with our unrealized desires. Exploring your dreams and fantasies can help you realize what you really want and need from life. Once a desire becomes conscious, you can work toward achieving it. God expects us to dream big; that's why he gave us an imagination. But he also expects us to get off our butts and do something. He won't do all the work, but he will provide the vision to see what we want and show us the pathway to get it done.

What are your dreams? What would you like to be doing five years from now?

1.

2.

3.

Of course, for most of us these dreams won't just fall into our laps. We have to focus on what we want and be diligent in our efforts to get there. Having big dreams isn't a problem if you're willing to plan ahead, focus, and work hard. Sometimes it's easy to set your dream aside when you feel there's so much time and space between your dreams and reality. **NEVER GIVE UP** on your dreams. I realize now that the only way my dreams will become reality is through hard work, faith, and "stick-to-it-ness." I include my dreams in my prayers, because I realize everything I do is based on my relationship with God.

Cherish Your Dreams.

I think dreams should be cherished like family heirlooms held close to our hearts. Dreams allow us to be free and give us peace. We can do all things through Christ, who strengthens us. Here's my favorite recipe for success

- 1 cup faith
- 1 teaspoon of hope
- ½ stick of imagination
- 2 cups of "stick-to-it-ness"

Mix all ingredients together, blend well, and add a foundation of creativity to the bottom of the pan so it will stick. Set your mind at 400 and let it cook for 20 to 25 minutes. Serve while warm.

Are Your Dreams Within Reach?

Sometimes dreams are so grand that they seem unattainable no matter how hard we work. A man digging ditches alongside the road sees a Mercedes limousine go by and dreams of owning that car and the lifestyle that goes with it. A woman who lives in a studio apartment dreams of a lovely estate in the country. Are these impossible dreams?

That depends. Consider this dialogue from Lewis Carroll's *Alice in Wonderland*:

> "I can't believe that!" said Alice.
> "Can't you?" the Queen said in a pitying tone. "Try again: draw a long breath and shut your eyes."
> Alice laughed. "There's no use trying," she said. "One can't believe in impossible things."
> "I daresay you haven't had much practice," said the Queen. "When I was your age, I always did it for half an hour a day. Why sometimes I've believed as many as six impossible things before breakfast."

Just sit quietly with your dream and make it seem like a real experience. Your subconscious mind can't distinguish a real experience from an imaginary one, so the things you dream about will become your inner reality. Then it's time to take that inner vision and move it to the outer world. What are some actions you can take now to help obtain your dream for the future?

1.

2.

3.

Did you know that the goal-setting and dreaming part of your mind is different from the part of your mind that achieves goals? Once you've set a goal for yourself, learn to turn it over to the "achieving" section of your brain.

Remember, if you see life in all its fullness, life will see you the same way. If you view life as limited, then life sees you as limited. If you dream big dreams you can have big realities. But it also takes "stick-to-it-ness, self-motivation, self assurance, determination, and 100% commitment to bring your passion to reality. Hard work, sacrifice, and a great deal of self discipline will be required. But you can do it, just step up, step out and let's go!

A Dream is a Wish Your Heart Makes

A dream is a wish your heart makes
When you're fast asleep.
In dreams you will lose your heartaches
Whatever you wish for, you keep.
Have faith in your dreams and someday,
Your rainbow will come smiling through.
No matter how your heart is grieving,
If you keep on believing,
The dream that you wish will come true.

By Mack David, Al Hoffman, Jerry Livingstone

Let's Get Back to Basics

I remember when I was young and growing up in a small town; it felt like everyone cared about everyone else. When someone was sick we automatically took food and helped out. Parents seemed to take time for their children and not just letting computer games or television raise them. There was a connected feeling that we've lost today. We've become so busy taking care of ourselves that we forget about the people around us. There was a collectiveness that seems to hold the community together.

Maybe it's just a matter of getting our priorities straight and finding our happy place, the place that gives us the most peace. Maybe it's time for us to stop doing things that make us unhappy and seek new challenges in our lives. But this also means we have to stop using excuses and blaming everyone else for our problems.

What if we could just get back to basics? I feel our lives should be adjusted to include our children and extended families. When I think of basics, I think of caring and sharing, sitting on the porch drinking tea, just enjoying the day. I think of low stress and plenty of rest. I think of looking at life as though each day is my last. If I could just live with this kind of peace, I know I'd be one step closer to heaven.

Reaching this goal may require giving up a few things, not having everything we **want,** but gaining what we **need**.

What we <u>want</u> and what we <u>need</u> are two different things

It's easy to confuse needs and wants, yet the two are not the same. Needs are things we must have in order to survive. Wants are the extra things we crave. Food, clothing, and shelter are needs. Gourmet food, designer clothing, and palatial houses are wants. When we get confused and put wants before needs, our lives can become stressful and chaotic. Make a list of the things you need in order to survive:

1.
2.
3.
4.
5.
6.
7.

Today we mainly worry over our wants rather than our needs. Take a look at the list you've made. Are all these items necessary? Do any of them fall into the spiritual category? Did you list your family and friends? Remember, we can shop every day, spend money on trinkets, and get instant gratification, but our internal need for love and connection will still be there. It won't go away. And don't forget physical health. Taking care of our bodies now will help ensure a vibrant and active life as we grow older. Here's a sample list of needs:

Food, Clothing, Shelter, Transportation (optional), Love, Health, Sufficient Income.

Do you already have everything you need? Are you content with your life? It's important to look at our needs and determine how many of them really are wants. I remember my daughter saying, "Mom, I need . . ." I would answer her by saying, "Don't say you need something, say you want it badly." She would rephrase her request, but she knew the word "need" sounded so much better than "want." "Need" makes us perk up and listen; it makes us try and figure out ways to get something. The goal of advertising is to convince us that we <u>need</u> the product being sold, whether it's a new toilet bowl cleaner or a diamond ring.

I've seen many cases where people's wants cancelled out their needs. I remember a friend who was determined to move in with a certain young man who had a nice apartment. Once she started living there, she realized her wants completely cancelled out her need to save money, because she was carrying most of the financial burden for an expensive place to live. In the end she developed a budget, found a small apartment of her own, and focused on her need to save money. She's now a very successful young lady and has decided the next time she lives with someone it will be a lifelong commitment.

I had another friend who divorced early in life, but felt she should be married. She really WANTED to be married, but after she remarried, this woman realized her relationship was more a want than a need. She was happier living alone and realized she'd lacked the patience to wait for God to bring the right man into her life.

God will provide all our needs. It's when we get involved with our wants that we redefine our needs and ignore God's plan for us.

When I was younger, my extended family taught me a lot by their actions. My uncle who lived across the street never went to college, but he was one of the best architects in town. He could build a perfect house from the ground up. He built three houses of his own and left one for each of his kids. He was rich in wisdom, but slow with words. He was strong in his faith and demonstrated this by the way he lived. I still remember his prayers on Sunday morning. He sent all his kids to college, recognizing the need for an education even though he didn't have one.

My grandmother was a maid all her life. She's very smart and always has good advice – even if you'd rather not hear it! She sent six kids to college on a maid's salary, yet I wonder how I'll send two at the same time. This woman understands the difference between needs and wants. She knows what's important in life.

Now, I realize the economy is different these days and things cost more, but the basic foundation and focus of life should be the same, **God, Family, Work** etc... We just need to get back to basics. .

Simplify your life

Achieving simplicity in our lives is one of the best ways to get back to basics. One way to do this is by evaluating what you do with your time. Are you spending hours every day trying to get things you <u>want</u> but don't <u>need</u>? Have you evaluated what you need to do with your time, versus things that simply clutter up your life? List three activities you'd like to get rid of:

1.
2.
3.

Now list the things that matter most to you:

1.
2.
3.
4.
5.

Perhaps you listed spending time with your family, achieving more at work, having time to travel, or maintaining your health. Here are a few ways to maximize time and simplify your life:

- Make a list of goals you'd like to achieve. Focus on doing a few things well instead of doing many things halfway.
- Learn to say no!
- Cut back the time you spend on meaningless activities, such as playing computer games and watching television.
- Spend more time with people who make positive contributions to your life. Spend less time with people who drain your energy. Get rid of negative influences.
- Do something each day to help someone else.
- Take time each day to enjoy nature, relax, and feel grateful for what you have.

Think of more ways to simplify your life. Following this plan will help create the peace and stability you need to achieve your goals. Many people have what they <u>want</u> in material goods, but they still aren't content because they don't have what they <u>need</u> spiritually and emotionally. I learned from my uncle and grandmother that it doesn't take a lot of material wealth to lead a happy, productive life. Their strength still gives me courage. In fact, they were models of strength, determination, and faith. They were encouraging and uplifting.

We should keep things simple and stay close to the basic concepts of life. Never lose sight of your dreams!

We are happy in proportion to the things we can do without.

Henry David Thoreau.

Simplicity is making the journey of this life with just enough baggage.

Anonymous

Be content with what you have, rejoice in the way things are. When you realize there is nothing lacking, the whole world belongs to you.

Lao Tzu

We don't need to increase our goods nearly as much as we need to scale down our wants. Not wanting something is as good as possessing it.

Donald Horban

Restricted for readers under 18

For Under 18 Only

Now, I realize you don't want to read a lot of boring advice about what to do with your life. Being a teenager or a kid these days isn't easy partly because you have so many options, some good and some bad. Technology is so advanced that you have the ability to learn almost anything that interests you. But new technology can't replace the basic things in life that will be important when you become an adult.

Believe in yourself

You have to believe in yourself before anyone one else will. Try to develop self-motivation. Don't always be motivated by something or someone else, because once that person's influence is gone from your life, who will get you going?

Be determined and willing to work hard for what you want. My son is 14 and plays football well. He's very determined and works hard in every game. If you're going to be involved in something, make sure you are giving it 150%; don't make others pick up the slack for you.

Have expectations for yourself and others. If you set high goals and expectations for yourself, you'll attract friends who also have high expectations. Set limits, set goals, and go for it. When you're taking a test and you have studied long and hard, expect to get an A. Expect to be the best and you will be.

FOCUS

Where you focus is where you'll go

If you focus on good, positive things, the results will be positive. If you focus on negative things you'll only get negative things back. For example, if you play competitive sports and you don't play to win, why bother playing at all? If you focus on doing things that will harm your life, this will produce a domino affect on your family and bring them down as you bring yourself down. Success is determined by aiming high, to get high results.

Who you're around is who you become:

You should be careful who you choose to hang with. Just because the crowd is popular doesn't mean they're good people. Choose your friends carefully and make sure you're still your own person, even with your friends. Don't get wrapped up in the wrong things. And I know you know what I mean!

Drugs can impair your for life forever and can kill you. Alcohol and cigarettes are fun now, but they're habit forming. The main thing about a habit is that it's easy to start and extremely difficult to break. Be mature and make the people in your life proud by just saying no! It's okay to be the odd man out. At least you'll be the one standing when you graduate.

Also, please know that sex is something you shouldn't have until you are married. I want all you young ladies to know that YOU CAN say NO and still be popular. If the guy you're with can't accept that and goes off with someone else, then you're better off anyway.

Also, bringing a child into the world at a young age is terribly difficult, as some of you already know. However, I want you to know that if you made this mistake in the past, just remember the past is over. You made a big mistake, but these are learning experiences that will help you grow and make you stronger. Mistakes are how we learn and grow. We just don't want to keep repeating the same mistakes, because that means we aren't learning or growing. You never want to get the reputation of being easy, because it's a hard reputation to change. Be aware of the relationships you choose and don't risk your life for 2 minutes of pleasure.

You can get diseases from unprotected sex that will cause a life time of despair, and maybe even take your life. You must be very careful. The best way to keep yourself healthy is just not to do it.

Guys you should know that treating a young lady with respect is to be commended. Maybe you'd rather be labeled a player than a gentleman, but remember the future. We really need more young men who will step up and take an active role in showing others how to be gentlemen with strong morals and character.

I often tell people ,in my workshops, that just because you drive the get-a-way car while your friends rob the bank doesn't mean you aren't guilty of robbing the bank. You're guilty by association. Remember, when someone's doing something wrong, you should get as far away from them as possible. You don't want to be around anything that will give you guilt by association.

Education

Oh, no, another lecture on education! I just want you to remember that the foundation you lay today determines what kind of building you'll live in later in life. A weak foundation equals a weak building; a strong foundation creates a strong building. Which do you prefer?

Knowledge is power, it will unlock doors throughout your life and bring you privileges and honor. Strive to be your best. Look forward to college or some other type of education. Remember you'll only be a kid for 18 years, but you'll be an adult for a lot longer, so begin preparing now for your future.

Respect

Webster's defines respect as: "to consider worthy of high regard."

Respect yourself and others, live a life you can be proud of. Work hard and have fun, but not at anyone else's expense.

I recently had a lady commend my son for saying "yes ma'am to her. She said, "You just don't hear that very often anymore." Now, I'm not telling you to say "yes ma'am" and "yes sir," but if you lived with me, I'd expect it. I believe you should give the proper respect to your elders and those who made it possible for you to have the things you enjoy today. That means anyone who's over 21. I still say "yes ma'am" and "yes sir" to people I meet. And some reply, "You don't have to say that, it makes me feel old," but this is a habit I find hard to break.

Respect your parents or guardians. As long as they aren't doing anything illegal or abusive and they're working hard to ensure you have the best of life, then you should show them respect. Good parents will ask where you've been and who you were with, and they need to know these things in order to protect you. They should tell you when to come and go; it's their job to know where you are. They also have every right to inquire about your grades and your homework, even if some of this information is embarrassing to you now. It's better to be a little embarrassed now than to fail a grade or class because you just didn't want to admit you were having trouble. My kids make good grades in school, but they had to learn the hard way that keeping something from me or their father will not result in good things. If they tell us and we can help, we all chalk it up as a mistake and we move on. I always tell my kids that everything will come out in the wash.

You only get one mom and dad, or one guardian. Don't misuse this special privilege God has granted you. Now look, I realize not all parents do a good job, and that's very unfortunate, but not all kids are good kids either. We must not follow bad examples no matter who it is. I'm not sure where grown people got the saying, "Just do as I say, not as I do." Nothing could be more wrong.

Work hard at not talking back; don't stay out late without a phone call. Don't get into trouble at school, or and always make an effort at doing your homework and study. Failure gets easier every time you do it. Success gets "sweeter" every time you do it. Please communicate with your parents, tell them when you feel bad, when someone has wronged you, or even when you think you're attracted to someone. I know you think that will be gross, but communication is the key to healthy relationships.

What you put in you get out:

If you don't have anyone monitoring what you watch and what you get into on the computer, you're going to have to rely on your gut. You know the voice inside that says, "You shouldn't do that." Turn it off or change the channel! Only chat

64

with people you know; don't go on the internet and look at things that will mess up your life.

I just want to say to all of you, I love kids and I wish I could rescue every child who's being misused and abused. Everyone deserves the chance to grow up and maybe become president someday or the best NFL or NBA player of all time. But mostly I believe all kids should have a chance to experience the good things in life, all the blessings God has in store.

So, if you know you aren't trying as hard as you can, change that now. If you know you haven't given life everything it has given you, change now. Don't talk about it with anyone, **just do it**. If you are not honoring your parents the way you should, change that now because you only get one time to be a kid or a teenager, so make the best of it and leave a good impression on the people who've helped mold you and make you in to the beautiful person you are today. Tell your parents you care about them and you appreciate all the hard work they do.

Life is not fair or unfair. I know kids and teenagers use those terms a lot, but in the end life is exactly what you make it. Be a kid, live life to the absolute fullest and know that today kids are really experiencing a lot of things. Stay cool, and stay young as long as you can. You are somebody and it is a privilege to have you read my chapter for 18 and under.

The Quicksand of Life
After Thoughts

Have you ever been walking through life, minding your own business, when the dirt under your feet suddenly feels soft and mushy? Soon that dirt begins to pull you under. Before you know it, your shoes are no longer on top of the ground. Confused, you try to pick up your feet, but they're stuck in the mud. Panic sets in as you struggle to free your self.

The harder you fight to break free, the further you sink into the quicksand. Desperate, you look around for help, but there's nothing to hold onto, nothing to grab; it's just you and the sand. Your life begins to flash before your eyes.

Just when you think all is lost and you'll disappear forever into this black hole, something grabs your arm and gradually draws you back onto solid ground. Looking around in disbelief, you find there's no one around. Who came to the rescue in your time of desperate need? It was God.

He is the protector of all, the doctor of the masses, the lawyer of the convicted, and the teacher of all those who'll listen. And in the midst of all these roles he holds us up, never letting us hold onto him; for he knows his children will stray.

It isn't unusual to feel as though the circumstances of life are pulling us down. Life's path is filled with quicksand traps: an undesirable relationship, disobedient children, tragedies in our lives, a drama-filled family, financial disasters, or a job that's out of control. The list could fill this page.

Have you considered asking for help? In the midst of our problems and tragedies, sometimes we become so overwhelmed by our own misery that we forget a higher power is available to help us. Some people call it God, and still others refer to a "higher power." No matter what you call it, there is loving energy available to us, and we don't have to wait until the quicksand is around our ears. We can use prayer as a regular part of our daily lives, for guidance, inspiration, and getting in touch with ourselves.

We each face two kinds of problems in our lives: troubles we bring upon ourselves through our own actions, and troubles life simply throws us out of the blue. Sometimes people believe suffering and tragedy means there's some hidden sin in their lives. But that just isn't so. Following a sin-free formula won't keep us from being persecuted, afflicted, sick, or in financial need. The trials and tribulations we face are part of life here on earth, and they will help us grow. One phrase I've found helpful when I face the quicksand of life is, "What doesn't kill you makes you stronger." By overcoming your troubles you gain knowledge and wisdom that makes you a better person and helps you handle the next set of problems life throws your way.

Many people learn best by experience, and sometimes we only learn certain lessons by getting burned. Later, these tough experiences can help us give counsel to others. No one can help others more than someone who's been through the same trial.

One of the most important things to remember about life's problems is that how we respond to trouble is more important than the trouble itself. Our responses reveal our innermost character. You may cruise along for years, being healthy, happy, and prosperous is every way. Everything seems ideal. But then the storms of life come and your values are put to the test. The Bible contains many examples of people whose lives seemed perfect until the bottom fell out.

The best way you can respond to a problem is by letting it move you closer to God instead pushing you further away. When we're hurt, we naturally want to turn to our parents for help, and in the same way we should go to God with all problems and trials. The more we call upon God in our lives, the more He'll be available to us. Becoming bitter and angry with God will only make things worse in our lives.

We can't always trust in our own wisdom to solve the troubles of life. There comes a point when we must totally entrust ourselves to a higher power. He may not take away the hard road, but he will give you strength to make the journey. Once you've made the journey yourself, you can help others along the way.

Make a list of your blessings, (you may need to get more paper.)

1.

2.

3.

4.

5.

Thinking on these things when you're troubled will help you remember the good things in life. God can, and often does, intervene in the lives of His children. There is no problem He cannot solve. He knows what you need in life, when you need it, and why you need it. Don't let the quicksand pull you down! Keep your head up, depend on God, and keep the faith. He is your anchor and salvation. Grab onto him and don't let go. Remember, **this too shall pass**.

Conclusion

Often in my groups I tell everyone, "Plan your work and work your plan." I'm sure they've heard that advice before, but it's still true. If you create a plan that can't be executed, why bother having a plan at all? Write down your goals in life. If you don't put them in writing it's like wandering through the grocery store without a list.

Remember, life is neither fair nor unfair, it's what you make it. Dream big and then make your dreams a reality. Be aware that your attitude about life is the key to unlocking the door of opportunity. Try to eliminate drama in your life, and always remember to take out the trash.

I leave you with my favorite story about myself: When I first moved to Houston, I heard a lot about the Galleria. Being a Type "A" personality, I didn't ask direction. I decided to just drive around until I found it. So, I got to a sign that said "610 Loop." I came from El Dorado, Arkansas, where we had one main street. So, I got on the 610 loop and started to drive . . . and . . . and drive. After awhile I began seeing the same things over and over again, so I knew something was wrong. I was on a loop. The most interesting thing about this is that at that time my entire life was "on a loop." I didn't know which exit to take or who to ask to get off that loop.

Sometimes we all loop in life. But we have to muster our courage, take an exit (any exit), and either ask for directions or buy a map at the nearest corner store. Remember, you may have passengers in the car and they're wondering if you know where you are going. Get off that loop and move toward the future!

Thanks to everyone for buying and reading my first book. I hope in some way I have encouraged you. May God continue to bless you.

About the Author

Jennifer Lynn Dean is President and founder of Dean's Professional Services, Inc., an award-winning medical staffing, consulting and leadership development firm. Jennifer graduated from the University of Houston with a bachelor's degree in Political Science and a minor in Sociology. She began her career in the medical arena 15 years ago. In 1993, Jennifer started her own medical company, specializing in medical staffing, staff development, and consulting.

The experience Jennifer has gained as a business owner in the medical industry has led to her strong desire to share her knowledge with others through public speaking and writing. A highly sought-after speaker, Jennifer speaks many times a year to various medical associations, physician's offices, educational centers, corporations and churches. Subjects she specializes in but are not limited to, are Healthcare Management, Customer Service, and Motivational Techniques.

Jennifer has also written articles on medical issues for the Houston Chronicle and a multitude of medical magazines. She is a member of Houston Society of Healthcare Human Resources Administration, where she serves on the board. In 1998, she was a finalist for the Pinnacle Awards and in 1999 and 2000, a finalist for the Ernst and Young's Entrepreneur of the Year Awards.

When speaking Jennifer shares what seems like a lifetime of insights, inspirations and aphorisms that will tickle your funny bone and challenge you to see customer service, internal and external, in a new light.

Jennifer lives in Katy, Texas with her husband Mike, and three kids Tiffany, Shannon, and Aundre.

For information on: Workshops, Seminars, or Keynote speaker:

Contact: Dean's Professional Services, Public

                 Relations Department

Phone number: 1-800-805-9318 / (713) 785-7483

Fax number: (713) 785-7601

Address: 6150 Richmond Ave #114

                 Houston, Texas 77057

To contact Jennifer Dean

E-mail: jdean@dpsinc-texas.com

         www.dpsinc-texas.com

Printed in the United States
29070LVS00007B/79-129